To all of our family and friends!

Riley has a new friend to share!

Their name is Benny and they are just a
cub of a bear,

They are smart, they are brave,
and they have a really neat chair!

Benny has even decorated it with some flare!

Riley is curious about Benny and their chair,

It's okay to ask in a way that's kind,
but it's impolite to stare.

Benny says their chair helps them
move and they are doing just fine!

Benny uses their legs
differently than yours or mine,

Sometimes cubs need help in their chair and others can do it themselves!

This isn't a chair with four legs but instead it has four wheels,

This doesn't take away
from the love they feel!

They play all kinds of games and sing
all the same songs,

They are so excited to go on
adventures with you,

Rolling or trotting there's
always something to do!

So, if you meet a friend that uses a
wheelchair Riley wants you to know,

Different isn't scary so let your friendship grow!

www.ingramcontent.com/pod-product-compliance
Lightning Source LLC
Chambersburg PA
CBHW042135110726

48006CB00003B/886